INVESTIGATING MYSTERIOUS PLACES

THE PARIS CATACOMBS

EMPIRE OF THE DEAD

by Scott Sonneborn

CAPSTONE PRESS
a capstone imprint

Published by Capstone Press, an imprint of Capstone
1710 Roe Crest Drive, North Mankato, Minnesota 56003
capstonepub.com

Library of Congress Cataloging-in-Publication Data is available on the Library of Congress website.

ISBN: 9781669093817 (hardcover)
ISBN: 9781669093763 (paperback)
ISBN: 9781669093770 (ebook PDF)

Summary: Step under the streets of Paris, France, to explore the Catacombs, an underground world of bones. Why are the bones of millions of people hidden beneath this famous city, and are there secrets still waiting to be uncovered in the so-called Empire of the Dead?

Editorial Credits
Editor: Donald Lemke; Designer: Tracy Davies; Media Researcher: Svetlana Zhurkin; Production Specialist: Katy LaVigne

Image Credits
Alamy: Cecile Marion, 8; Dreamstime: Dirk Wenzel, 6, Kristofbellens, 5; Getty Images: AFP/Miguel Medina, 9, 19, AFP/Patrick Kovarik, 24, Gamma-Rapho/Jean-Francois Deroubaix, 11, Paris Match/Manuel Litran, 27; Newscom: MAXPPP/Le Parisien/PhotoPQR, 25, Zuma Press/Cristian Leyva, 7; Shutterstock: AlexStnv, 26, Aliaksei Hintau (smoke background), 2 and throughout, Andrea Izzotti, 15, Delpixel, 17, dreamansions, cover, Everett Collection, 13, GarryKillian, 18, Irina Senkova, 29, JudeAnd, 21, Kirill Veprikov, 14, Mikhail Gnatkovskiy, 20, Vasilii Duda (skull and crossbones icon), cover and throughout; SuperStock: Image Asset Management/World History Archive, 23

TABLE OF CONTENTS

Chapter One

BONES UNDER THE STREETS

The Paris **Catacombs** are a series of underground tunnels that hold the remains of millions of dead people. But there are no coffins or graves in these tunnels. The bones are stacked right up against the walls!

In many of the tunnels, **skulls** and other bones have been placed to form strange shapes. They are stacked to look like barrels, circles, and even hearts.

The Barrel of Passion is a popular site inside the Catacombs.

That might sound creepy, but the Catacombs are a popular place to visit. Every year, more than 500,000 people tour there.

Visitors walk 131 steps from the streets of Paris, France, down into the Catacombs. They explore the many tunnels with help from guides.

People wait to enter the Catacombs in Paris.

FACT

Parisian quarry miners made the tunnels before they were used as cemeteries.

Many people visit only once. Others go again and again. These superfans are called **cataphiles**.

Many cataphiles enjoy the history of the underground tunnels. Some cover the walls in **graffiti** art. But all love exploring these tunnels full of human bones.

Chapter Two

THE BEGINNING

People began mining underneath Paris in the thirteenth century. They were digging for limestone. This rock was used to build some of Paris's most famous buildings.

Miners dug tunnels to get to the limestone. These tunnels sat empty for hundreds of years.

Limestone found in the Paris Catacombs is a distinct cream-gray color.

During that time, the city of Paris grew. Millions of people lived—and died—in the busy city. By the 1700s, the city's graveyards were **overcrowded**.

Many people throughout the city complained about the smell of death. Then in 1780, a huge rainstorm hit one of Paris's cemeteries.

FACT

Before the Catacombs, Paris's oldest and most used graveyard was called Holy Innocents' Cemetery.

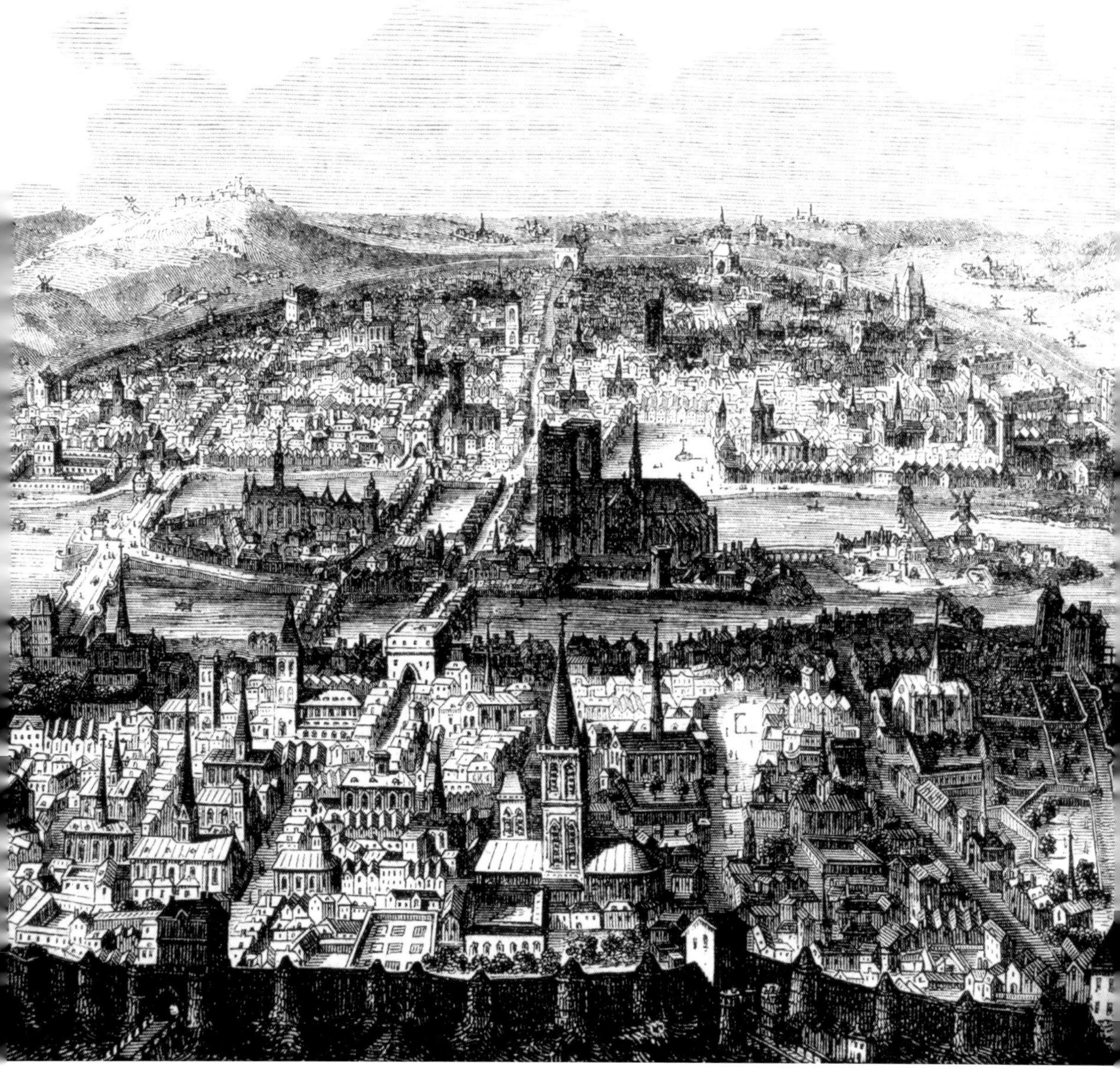

Paris, France, during the late 1700s

Dead bodies flowed out of their graves. They spilled into streets and people's homes. Something had to be done!

A marker for the bones from the Holy Innocents' Cemetery stacked in the Catacombs in 1809

Starting in 1785, people removed bones from the graveyards. They put them in the empty tunnels beneath Paris. During the next **decade**, bones from 6 million corpses were taken from graves and placed in the tunnels.

FACT

Some of the bones had been buried for 1,200 years before they were dug up and moved.

Chapter Three

VISITING THE CATACOMBS

At the entrance to the Paris Catacombs is a warning written in French. It reads, “Stop! This is the empire of death.” Still, millions of the living have gone down there since the Catacombs were opened to the **public** in 1809.

ARRETE!
C'EST ICI L'EMPIRE DE LA MORT

The Catacombs are five stories below the ground. Walking through the tunnels that are open to visitors takes about 45 minutes. But that's just a small part of the Catacombs.

Tunnels open to visitors are dimly lit by electric lights.

Visitors explore forbidden areas of the Paris Catacombs.

In all, the tunnels run back and forth under Paris for 170 miles (274 kilometers). If you add up all the space in the Catacombs, it totals almost 3 acres (1.2 hectares). That's enough room for two football fields!

The tunnels in the Paris Catacombs are very **narrow**. In some places, a person can touch both walls if they stretch out their arms!

The tunnel ceilings are low. A tall person might need to duck. It's also dark down there, and the lights make shadows dance on the walls.

Chapter Four

MYSTERIES REMAIN

The Paris Catacombs are hidden deep underground. They are the perfect place for secret meetings.

Some people in France met in the tunnels during World War II (1939–1945). They were part of a group called the French **Resistance**. They made plans to fight against Nazi Germany.

Members of the French Resistance meet in the Paris Catacombs, 1944.

In 2004, officials discovered that someone had built a secret movie theater in the Catacombs. The theater had seating for 30 people, a bar, and a restaurant.

French police patrol the Catacombs for unlawful visitors and activities.

The movie theater even had a working bathroom! All of that was hidden in a tunnel behind a "No Access" sign.

FACT

The underground tunnels near the Catacombs have pools of water. Despite the danger, some people swim in them!

People sometimes get lost in the Catacombs. In 2017, two teenagers were lost down there for three days! But that's nothing compared to what happened to Philibert Aspairt.

A tombstone honoring Philibert Aspairt in the Paris Catacombs

In 1793, Aspairt got lost in the Catacombs for 11 years! By the time he was found by a group of cataphiles, he had died—one more body among the 6 million there.

The Catacombs hold many secrets under the streets of Paris. It's a spooky place but also one filled with mysteries. Who knows what other stories the bones could tell us?

Glossary

catacombs (KAT-uh-kohmz)—underground tunnels or passages, especially those used as burial places

cataphile (KAT-uh-fyl)—a person who is enthusiastic about exploring and visiting the Catacombs, often fascinated by its history and mysteries

decade (DEH-kayd)—a period of 10 years

graffiti (gruh-FEE-tee)—usually unlawful writing or drawing on a public surface

narrow (NAYR-oh)—of less than usual, or slender, width

overcrowded (oh-ver-KROW-did)—filled with too many people or things, beyond the capacity of what is normal or suitable

public (PUHB-lik)—the people as a whole

resistance (ri-ZIS-tuhns)—the act of opposing or fighting against something, often in a secretive or underground manner

skull (SKUHL)—the case of bone or cartilage that forms the skeleton of the head and face

Read More

Carlson-Berne, Emma. *Haunted History.* Minneapolis: Lerner Publications, 2023.

Doeden, Matt. *Could You Escape the Paris Catacombs?: An Interactive Survival Adventure.* North Mankato, MN: Capstone, 2019.

Makin, Patrick. *The World's Most Mysterious Places.* New York: Abrams, 2020.

Internet Sites

Atlas Obscura: Catacombes de Paris
atlasobscura.com/places/catacombes-de-paris

History.com: The Dark Origins of the Paris Catacombs
history.com/news/paris-catacombs-origins

Le Catacombes de Paris: The Paris Catacombs
catacombes.paris.fr/en

Index

About the Author

Scott Sonneborn is the author of more than 40 books for kids. He's also written a bunch of TV shows and been nominated for both an Emmy and a Hugo Award. He lives in Los Angeles with his wife and their two sons.